June 14, 1998
Happy Birthday
and
many blessings.
Love,

Lisa & Rolando

# Prayers
# and
# Meditations

## From Around
## the World

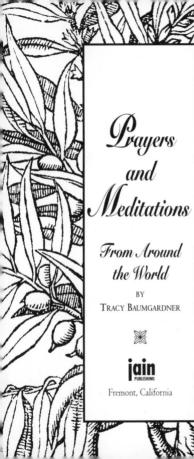

# Prayers and Meditations

## From Around the World

BY
TRACY BAUMGARDNER

## jain
PUBLISHING

Fremont, California

ISBN 0-87573-065-5

Printed in China

# Table of Contents

# Introduction

As one can ascend to the top of a house by means of a ladder, or a bamboo, or a staircase, or a rope, so diverse are the ways and means to approach God, and every religion in the world shows one of these ways.

*Ramakrishna Paramahansa*

The faiths of all others deserve to be honored for one reason or another. By honoring them, one exalts one's own faith and at the same time performs a service to the faiths of others. . . . If a man extols his own faith and disparages another because of devotion to his own and because he wants to glorify it, he seriously injures his own faith.

*King Asoka*

We have lost the concept of a supreme complete entity which used to restrain our passions and irresponsibility. We have placed too much hope in political and social reforms, only to find out that we were being deprived of our most precious possession: our spiritual life. . . . No one on earth has any other way left but inward.

*Aleksandr Solzhenitsyn*

# Creation

There is no birth, nor is there death; there is no beginning, nor is there any ending; nothing is identical with itself, nor is there any diversification; nothing comes into existence, nor does anything go out of existence.

*Buddhist Doctrine*

❋

In the beginning was God. Today is God, tomorrow will be God. Who can make an image of God? He has no body. He has a word which comes out of your mouth. That word! It is no more, it is past; and still it lives! So is God.

*Pygmy Hymn, Africa*

❋

The earth is the mother of us all.

*African Proverb, Uganda*

✳

His is the primacy over all created things, for in him were created all things in heaven and on earth; everything visible and everything invisible. Thrones, dominations, sovereignties, powers. All things were created through him and for him. Before everything was created he existed. And he holds all things in unity.

*St. Paul on Jesus*

✳

In the same way, when you accept the fact that all creation is a part of you, you can move it, you can get it to respond to you. That's why some of us can speak with the animals, and have them come to us when we call them. We can talk to the trees, to the earth, to the creator, and ask for what we need at a particular time.

*Sun Bear,* THE PATH OF POWER

✳

From the conception the increase, from the increase the thought, from the thought the remembrance, from the remembrance the consciousness, from the consciousness the desire. The world became fruitful; it dwelt with the feeble glimmering; it brought forth night: the long nights, the lowest night, the loftiest night, the thick night to be felt, the night to be touched; the night not to be seen, the night ending and death. From the nothing the begetting, from the nothing the increase, from the nothing the abundance, the power of increasing, the living breath.

*Maori Tribe, New Zealand*

$H$e (God) of whom the sky, the earth and the atmosphere, are woven, and the mind, together with all the life-breath, He alone knows as the one Soul. Other words dismiss, He is bridge to immortality.

*Tahitian Creationism*

※

$I$n the beginning God created the heavens and the earth. And the earth was formless and void, and darkness was over the surface of the deep; and the spirit of God was moving over the surface of the waters. Then God said, "Let there be light," and there was light.

THE BIBLE

※

$H$ow mistaken I was! How mistaken I was! Raise the screen and see the world! If anyone asks me what philosophy I understand, I'll straightaway give him a blow across his mouth with my hossu (hand).

*Chokei, Zen Monk*

※

14

From the everlasting I was firmly set, from the beginning, before the earth came into being. The deep was not when I was born. There were no springs to gush with water. Before the mountains were settled, before the hills, I came to birth, I came forth from the mouth of the Most High and I covered the earth like a mist. I had my tent in the heights, and my throne in a pillar of a cloud. Alone I encircled the vault of the sky. And I walked on the bottom of the deep, over the waves of the sea and over the whole earth, and over every people and nation I have held sway. Approach me, you who desire me, and take your fill of my fruits. Those who eat me will hunger for more. And they who drink me will thirst for more.

*Mother Goddess, 300 BC*

# Prayers
## to the Great Spirit

The way to ascend into God is to descend into one's self.

*Zen Saying*

✳

God [has] no father, nor mother, nor wife, nor children; He is neither a child nor an old man; He is the same today as he was yesterday.

*Gikuyu Tribe , Africa*

✳

The Lord gives wisdom; from His mouth comes knowledge and understanding.

THE BIBLE

✳

Thou art the fire, Thou art the sun, Thou art the air. . . Thou art the moon, Thou art the starry firmament. Thou art Brahma supreme. Thou art the waters. . . Thou art the creator of all. Thou art woman, Thou art man; Thou art the old man tottering with his staff. Thou art faces everywhere. Thou art the dark butterfly. Thou art the green parrot with the red eyes. Thou art the thunder cloud, the season, the seas. Without beginning, art Thou, beyond time, beyond space.

THE UPANISHADS

※

God Sends Lightning to strike the one he wants to be his slave in heaven.

*African Proverb*

※

There exists but one God, who is called the true, the creator, free from fear and hate, immortal, not begotten, self-existent, great and compassionate. The true was at the beginning, the true was at the distant past. The true is at the present, O Nanak, the true will also be in the future.

*Guru Nanak's Hymn, Sikh Faith*

❋

To me God is truth and love; God is ethics and morality; God is fearlessness; God is the source of the light and life; and yet He is above and beyond all these. God is consciousness.

*Mahatma Gandhi*

❋

God is so high you can't get above him. God is so low you can't get beneath him. God is so wide you can't get around him. You'd better come in by the gate.

*African American Spiritual*

❋

O Great Spirit, whose voice I hear in the winds, and whose breath gives life to all the world, hear me. I am small and weak, I need your strength and wisdom. Let me walk in beauty, and make my eyes ever behold the red and purple sunset. Make my hands respect the things you have made and my ears sharp to hear your voice. Make me wise so that I may understand the things you have hidden in every leaf and rock. I seek strength, not to be greater than my brother, but to fight my greatest enemy, myself. Make me always ready to come to you with clean hands and straight eyes. So when life fades, as the fading sunset, my spirit may come to you without shame.

*American Indian Prayer*

✳

Blue evening falls. Blue evening falls. Nearby in every direction it sets the corn tassels trembling.

*Papago Indians*

✳

And now in these thy dispensations, O God! Do thou wisely act for us, and with abundance with thy bounty and thy tenderness as touching us; and grant that reward which thou appointed to our souls, O God! Of this do thou thyself bestow upon us for this world and the spiritual; and now part thereof do thou grant and we may attain to fellowship with thee and thy righteousness for all duration.

*Zoroastrian Faith*

Allah is the light of the heavens and the earth. His light may be compared to a niche that enshrines a lamp, the lamp within a crystal of star-like brightness. It is lit from a blessed olive tree neither eastern nor western. Its very oil would almost shine forth, though no fire touched it. Light upon light: Allah guides to his light whom he will.

THE QUR'AN

Thou has vouchsafed, O Te (God) to hear from us. Thy child, dull and unenlightened, I am unable to show forth my dutiful feelings. I thank thee, that thou has accepted the intimation. With reverence we spread out these gems and silks, and as swallows rejoicing in the spring, praise thy abundant love.

*Taoist Prayer*

Wherever I am, wherever I go, I can sense something of the power of God. The grandeur of the mountains, the vastness of the oceans . . . all this proclaims the glory of God. Even amid the clutter of our cities built and abused by men, there are reflections of divine splendor. Heaven's silence or earth's clamor may not be very articulate, yet God's voice can be heard. . . . He makes his presence known.

THE BIBLE

At the gates of the transcendent stands that mere and perfect spirit described in the Upanishads, luminous, pure, sustaining the world, without flaw of duality, without the sear of division, transcendent silence.

*Sri Aurobindo*

※

Praise be to Allah, Lord of the worlds, the beneficent, the merciful, master of Judgement Day, You do we worship and You we beseech for help; guide us on the right path, the path of those whom You have favored, and not of those upon whom You have brought down your wrath, and who have gone astray.

*The Al-Fattah, Call to Worship*

※

Those who know don't talk about it; those who talk don't know.

TAO TE CHING

※

Thou art eternal among eternals, the consciousness within all minds, the unity in diversity, the end of all desiring. Understanding and experience of thee dissolve all limitations.

THE UPANISHADS

✳

He is Allah, besides whom there is no other god. He is the sovereign Lord, the holy one, the giver of peace, the keeper of faith; the guardian, the mighty one, the all-powerful, the most high! Exalted be He above their idols! He is Allah, the creator, the originator, the modelor. His are the gracious names; all that is in heaven and earth gives glory to Him; He is the might, the wise one.

THE QUR'AN

✳

I am Atum, I who was alone, I am Re at his
first appearance. I am the great God, self-gener-
ator, who fashioned his names, Lord of gods,
whom none approaches among the gods. I was
yesterday, I know tomorrow. The battlefield of
the gods was made when I spoke. I know the
name of that great God who is therein. "Praise
of Re" is his name. I am that great Phoenix
which is in Heliopolis (heaven).

*Inscription on Egyptian Tomb*

Holy Temple.
Here even a snake sheds
its earthly skin.

*Buddhist Poem*

# Gathering Faith

Do you need proof of God? Does one light a torch to see the sun?

*Chinese Proverb*

✴

In the day of my trouble I sought God with my hands lifted up to him in the night, and I was not deceived. My soul remembered God, and was delighted, and was exercised, and my spirit swooned away.

THE BIBLE

✴

Let nothing upset you; let nothing frighten you. Everything is changing; God alone is changeless. Patience attains the goal. Who has God lacks nothing. God alone fills all our needs.

*Saint Thérèse de Lisieux*

✴

Have you not known? Have you not heard? The Lord is the everlasting God, the creator of the ends of the earth. He does not faint or grow weary, his understanding is unsearchable. He gives power to the faint, and to him who has not might he increases strength. Even youths shall faint and be weary, and young men shall fall exhausted; but they who wait for the Lord shall renew their strength, they shall mount up with wings like eagles, they shall run and not be weary, they shall walk and not faint.

THE BIBLE

※

I used to pray that God would do this or that. Now I pray that God will make His will known to me.

*Mme Chiang Kai-chek*

※

If God created shadows, it was in order to better emphasize the light.

*Pope John XXIII*

※

I believe in the sun even when it is not shining,
I believe in love even when not feeling it.
I believe in God even when He is silent.

*Inscription on a Cologne Cellar*
*where Jews hid from the Nazis during WWII*

❈

Which of you by worrying can add one cubit to his stature? And why do you worry about clothes? Consider the lilies of the field, how they grow; they toil not, neither do they spin; yet I say to you that even Solomon in all his glory was not arrayed like one of these. Wherefore, if God so clothe the grass of the field, which today is green and tomorrow is cast into the oven, will He not much more clothe you, O ye of little faith?

*Jesus*

❈

Faith is the bird that knows dawn
and sings while it is still dark.

*Tagore*

❈

When you come down to it, what is our wondering but worship? To worship is to admit worth. And to wonder at something with open mouth, incredulous eye and awestruck mind is to do the same. It is to get beneath the common husk of things, to get above the plodding levels on which we live. To wonder and to worship is to be ushered into the essence of God. So look up at the sky, look down at the earth, look around at our brothers, and wonder at the kingdom in which we live.

*The Reverend Weston A. Stevens*

As a man in prison suffering pain for long knows that there is no pleasure for him but only to await release, so you look upon your existences on earth as prison, and turn your face towards renunciation and await release.

THE THIRD PERFECTION, *Buddhist Faith*

If a man allies himself with (God) the (devil) will eventually be conquered. On that day, the Day of Judgement, a happy life will begin for all mankind.

*Zoroastrian Faith*

※

Be strong and of good courage; be not frightened, neither be dismayed; for the Lord your God is with you wherever you go.

THE BIBLE

※

Bestow upon me, O Lord my God, understanding to know thee, diligence to seek thee, and a faithfulness that may finally embrace thee.

*St. Thomas Aquinas*

※

Fishes, asking what water was, went to a wise fish. He told them that it was all around them, yet they still thought they were thirsty.

*Sufi Faith*

※

Whither thou goest, I will go; and where thou lodgest, I will lodge; thy people shall be my people, and thy God my God. Where thou diest, I will die, and there I will be buried; the Lord do so to me, and more also, if aught but death part thee and me.

*Ruth to Her Mother-in-Law Naomi*
THE BIBLE

※

Then I understand their end . . . You will guide me. . . . And afterward receive me to glory.

THE BIBLE

※

Alexander, Caeser, Charlemagne and I, have built great empires, but upon what did they depend? They depended on force. But centuries ago Jesus started an empire that was built on love, and even to this day millions will die for him.

*Napoleon Bonaparte*

※

O give thanks that spring will always come to make your heart leap, that your winter ear remembers a summer song, and autumn colors return to the jaded eye.

*Rabbi Chaim Stern*

※

F or our part, we have true peace and rest in the Lord in all our sufferings, and are made willing in the power and strength of God, freely to offer up our lives, in this cause of God for which we suffer, yearn; and we do find, through grace, the enlargement of God in our imprisoned estate, to whom alone we commit ourselves and families, for the disposing of us according to his infinite wisdom and pleasure, in whose love is our rest and life.

*Salem Quakers from Jail*

※

N ow faith is the substance of things hoped for, the evidence of things not seen.

THE BIBLE

※

# Living With a Peaceful Mind

Life is a tale told by an idiot,
full of sound and fury signifying nothing.

*William Shakespeare*

✻

As to the way—the intelligent man goes
beyond it, the imbecile does not go far enough.

*From the Chang Yong, 4*

✻

The bearer of evil tidings,
when he was halfway there,
remembered that evil tidings
were a dangerous thing to bear.

*Robert Frost*

✻

Being one, truth cannot be divided, and the differences that appear to exist among the many nations only result from their attachment to prejudice. If only men would search out the truth, they would find themselves united.

*Abdul'l-Baha', Bahai'i Faith*

�֎

He enters a battle gravely, with sorrow and with great compassion, as if he were attending a funeral.

TAO TE CHING

✷

If two parties of believers take up arms against the other, make peace between them. If either of them commits aggression against the other, fight against the aggressors till they submit to Allah's judgement. When they submit make peace between them in equality and justice.

THE QUR'AN

✷

Only the supremely wise and the abysmally ignorant do not change.

*Confucius*

❈

Both heaven and hell come from one's own heart.

*Shinto Faith*

❈

As the soft yield of water cleaves the obstinate stone, so to yield with life solves the insoluble;to yield, I have learned, is to come back again. But this unworded lesson, this easy example, is lost upon men.

Tao Te Ching

❈

The world reveals itself in beauty, dignity and simplicity.

*Shinto Faith*

❈

The truth is no one knows me. I do not accuse heaven nor lay the blame on men. Below are felt on high, and perhaps after all I am known not here but in heaven.

*Confucius*

Happiness is neither within us only, or without us; it is the union of ourselves with God.

*Blaise Pascal*

The Lord gives wisdom; from His mouth comes Knowledge and understanding.

The Bible

If I am not for myself, who will be for me?
If I am only for myself what am I?
If not now; when?

*Rabbi Hillel, Mishnah, Jewish Faith*

A man should always be soft as a reed and not hard, like a cedar.

✺

Patience is power; with time and patience the Mulberry leaf becomes silk.

*Chinese Proverb*

✺

The ritual of the one who has seen the Shah (God) is above anger and kindness, infidelity and religion.

MATHNAWI

✺

I am the light of the world: he that followeth me shall not walk in darkness but shall have the light of life.

THE BIBLE

✺

Put your hands to work and your hearts to God.

*Mother Ann Lee, Shaker Faith*

※

This is your new hut; you desire another new hut. Discard the hope of a hut; a new hut will be painful again, monk.

*Buddhist Faith*

※

A mind that is fast is sick, a mind that is slow is sound, a mind that is still is divine.

*Meher Baba*

※

One to me is loss or gain, one to me is fame or shame, one to me is pleasure, pain.

BHAGAVAD-GITA

※

My life is my message.

*Gandhi*

※

40

And seeing the multitudes, he went up into a mountain: and he opened his mouth and taught them saying: Blessed are the poor in spirit; for theirs is the kingdom of heaven. Blessed are they that mourn; for they shall be comforted. Blessed are the meek; for they shall inherit the earth. Blessed are they which do hunger and thirst after righteousness; they shall be filled. Blessed are the merciful; for they shall obtain mercy. Blessed are the pure in heart; for they shall see God. Blessed are the peacemakers; for they shall be called the children of God. Blessed are they which are persecuted for righteousness sake; for theirs is the kingdom of heaven. Blessed are ye, when men shall revile you, and persecute you, and shall say all manner of evil against you falsely, for my sake. Rejoice and be exceedingly glad: for great is your reward in heaven; for so persecuted they the prophets which were before you.

*Jesus*

The sky rains melodiously. My small hut is roofed, pleasant, draught-free, and my mind is well concentrated. So rain, sky, if you wish.

*Buddhist Faith*

❋

A flower standing quietly by the fence, you smile your wondrous smile. I am speechless, and my senses are filled by the sounds of your beautiful song, beginning and endless. I bow deeply to you.

*Thich Nhat Hanh*

❋

Be not conformed to this world; but be ye transformed by the renewing of your mind.

THE BIBLE

❋

Happy is the man who cultivates the things that are hidden and lets the things that are apparent take care of themselves.

*Shinto Faith*

❋

The self is all knowing. It is all understanding, and to it belongs all glory. It is pure consciousness, dwelling in the heart of all, in the divine citadel of Brahma. There is no space it does not fill.

THE UPANISHADS

✳

I release all of my past, negatives, fears, human relationships, concept of self, my future and human desires to the light. I am a light being. I radiate the light from my light centers to everyone. I radiate light from my light centers to everything, I am in a bubble of light, and only light can come and only light can be here. Thank you God for everything, for everyone, and for me.

*New Age Meditation*

✳

As a solid rock is not shaken by the wind, so the wise man does not waver before blame or praise.

*Buddhist Tenet*

✳

As you practice meditation, you may see vision forms resembling snow, crystal, wind, smoke, fire, lightning, fireflies, the sun, the moon. These are the signs that you are on the way to the revelation of God.

THE UPANISHADS

�֎

A waterfall goes flying past the courtyard.
A lofty forest dazzles at the windows.
 In this house of meditation
we realize that all is void.
In this temple of debate
we analyze subtle Truths.

*Buddhist Poem*

✖

Breathing in, I calm my body. Breathing out, I smile. Dwelling in the present moment, I know this is a wonderful moment!

*Thich Nhat Hanh*

✖

If there be righteousness in the heart, there will be beauty in the character. If there be beauty in the character, there will be harmony in the home. If there be harmony in the home, there will be order in the nation. If there be order in the nation, there will be peace in the world.

*Confucius*

※

If you are quiet and tranquil you can become the ruler of the whole world.

TAO TE CHING

※

Observe all the white around you, but remember all the black that is there.

TAO TE CHING

※

When closely inspected,
one notices flowers in bloom
under the hedge!

*Basho*

※

45

$A$h, but a man's reach
should far exceed his grasp,
or what's a heaven for?

*Robert Browning*

❋

$I$t advantages a Brahman (holy person) not a
little if he holds his mind back from the allure-
ments of life; in direct measure as the wish to
injure declines, suffering is quieted.

*Buddhist Canon*

❋

$M$ay the God of hope fill you with all joy
and peace as you trust in Him, so that you may
overflow with hope by the power of the Holy
Spirit.

THE BIBLE

❋

$O$ne excellent way to practice the rules
of propriety is to be natural.

*Confucius*

❋

46

In order to have pleasure in everything, desire to have pleasure in nothing. In order to arrive at possessing everything, desire to possess nothing. In order to arrive at being everything, desire to be nothing. In order to know everything, desire to know nothing.

*St. John of-the-Cross*

✳

I will be happy forever!
Nothing will hinder me.
I walk with beauty before me.
I walk with beauty behind me.
I walk with beauty above me.
I walk with beauty below me.
I walk with beauty around me.
My words will be beautiful.

*Navaho Blessing*

✳

When he shows no preference in fortune or misfortune, neither exults or hates, his insight is sure. . . . Brooding about sensuous objects makes attachment to them grow. From attachment desire arises . . . from desire anger is born. When one renounces all desires and acts without cravings, possessiveness, or individuality, he finds peace.

THE BHAGAVAD-GITA

�֎

We should stop working and rushing around on Sunday, not just to rest so that we can start over again on Monday, but to collect our wits and to realize the relative meaninglessness of the secu-lar business that fills the other six days of the week.

*Thomas Merton, Catholic Monk*

✖

He who stands on tiptoe doesn't stand firm. He who rushes ahead doesn't go far. He who tries to shine dims his own light.

TAO TE CHING

✖

No need to leave your door to know the whole world; no need to peer through your windows to know the way of heaven. The farther you go, the less you know. Therefore the sage knows without going, names without seeing, and completes without doing a thing.

TAO TE CHING

My poems are poems
though some may call them sermons.
Poems and sermons are just alike,
they need to be read closely.
Go slow; open gently,
it's easy to miss the point.
Take poetry to be your guide
and you might find out
a lot of funny things.

*Buddhist Poem*

Humanitarianism consists of never sacrificing a human being to a purpose.

*Albert Schweitzer*

※

The five colors can blind, the five tones deafen, the five tastes cloy; the race, the hunt, can drive men mad, and their booty leave them no peace. Therefore the sensible man prefers the inner to the outer eye.

TAO TE CHING

※

Go straight to the pine trees to learn of pine and to bamboo stalks to know bamboo.

*Buddhist Saying*

※

This body is the true wisdom. The soul is like a mirror bright. Take heed to keep it always clean. And let no dust collect upon it.

*Zen Faith*

※

Come unto me, all ye that labour and are heavy laden, and I will give you rest. Take my yoke upon you and learn of me; for I am meek and lowly in heart; and ye shall find rest unto your souls. For my yoke is easy, and my burden is light.

THE BIBLE

❋

With clean water and wide crags,
haunted by monkey and deer,
covered with oozing moss,
These rocks delight me.

*Buddhist Poem*

❋

Nations and tribes of the world, who are always at war, turn your face towards unity and let the brightness of its light shine upon you.

*Baha'u'llah*

❋

Keep us, O God, from pettiness; let us be large in thought, word and deed. Let us be done with faultfinding and leave off self-seeking. May we put away all pretense, and meet each other, face to face, without self-pity and without prejudice. May we never be hasty in judgement and always generous. Let us take time for all things; make us grow calm, serene, gentle. Teach us to put in action our better impulses—straightforward and unafraid. Grant that we may realize it is the little things of life that create difficulty, that in the big things of life, we are as one. Imbue us with a deep and sincere love for others, O Holy Spirit.

*Mary, Queen of Scots, 1573*

Are you endeavoring to make your home a place of friendliness, refreshment and peace, where God becomes more real to all who dwell there and to all who use it?

*Society of Friends*

I am Apo (Spirit). Here we are, standing up and facing toward the sunrise, I am offering a prayer again asking your blessing. The sun you made has come up, it is shining toward us, all over, and it is the light from you, and we like to have this every day of our life, and we want to live a long time. Because we are suffering for our homes, families and friends, and all kinds of nations, I want you to bless us; and I ask you to bless the service boys so that they will be safe and nothing will happen to them. I ask you to see to it that there will be no war, make it that way through your will power.

*Soshoni Chief, Sundance Ceremony Prayer, 1945*

※

You have made us for yourself and our hearts are restless till they find their rest in You.

*St. Augustine*

※

# *The Ethical Way*

Work on your own realization with diligence.

*The Buddha*

Create in me a clean heart, O God; and renew a right spirit within me.

THE BIBLE

Truth is the first virtue.

*Zoroastrian Faith*

A child does not laugh at the ugliness of its mother.

*African Proverb, Uganda*

As the star of healing is balanced in the heavens, and swerves not from its path in its time and its seasons, so also shall you remain fixed in your path of truth.

*Buddhist Faith*

❈

Therefore thou art inexcusable, O man, whosoever thou art that judgest; for wherein thou judgest, thou condemnest thyself; for you that judgest doeth the same things.

<small>THE BIBLE</small>

❈

Fret not thyself because of evil doers, neither be thou envious against the workers of iniquity. For they shall be cut down like the grass, and wither as the green herb. Trust in the Lord, and do good; so shalt thou dwell in the land, and verily thou shalt be fed.

<small>THE BIBLE</small>

❈

I call God long suffering and patient precisely because he permits evil in the world. He is the author of it and yet untouched by it.

*Mahatma Gandhi*

※

Though He causes grief, He will show compassion according to the multitude of His mercies.

THE BIBLE

※

Those who would take over the earth, and shape it to their will, never, I notice, succeed. The earth is like a vessel so sacred that at the mere approach of the profane it is marred. And when they reach out their fingers it is gone!

TAO TE CHING

※

If men thought as much of God as they think of the world, who would not attain liberation?

THE UPANISHADS

※

You are the light of the world. A city set on a hill cannot be hid. Nor do men light a lamp and put it under a bushel, but on a stand, and it gives light to all who are in the house. Let your light so shine before men that they may see your good words and glorify your good works and glorify your father who is in heaven.

*Jesus*

❋

Let no man think lightly of evil, or say in his heart, it will not come nigh unto me. Even by the falling of water drops, a water pot is filled; the fool becomes full of evil, even if he gathers it, little by little.

*Buddhist Canon*

❋

First remove the plank from your own eye, and then you will see clearly.

THE BIBLE

❋

While they (the parents) are alive, serve them according to the ritual. When they die, bury them according to the ritual; and sacrifice to them according to the ritual.

*Confucius*

❋

Now to get rid of the lower self. The blossom vanishes of itself as the fruit grows, so will your lower self vanish as the divine grows in you.

*Ramakrishna Paramahansa*

❋

Do you have the patience to wait till your mud settles and the water is clear? Can you remain unmoving till the right action arises by itself?

Tao Te Ching

❋

Be ye therefore wise as serpents, and harmless as doves.

The Bible

❋

Purity is for man, next to life, the greatest good; that purity, O Zarathustra, that is in the religion of ours for him to cleanse his own self with good thoughts, deeds and words.

*Zoroastrian Faith*

🔸

Ye have heard it that it has been said, an eye for an eye and a tooth for a tooth: but I say unto you, that you resist not evil: but whosoever shall smite thee on thy right cheek, turn to him the other also.

THE BIBLE

🔸

Good implies the idea of evil; and beauty implies the idea of ugliness.

TAO TE CHING

🔸

Be not hasty in thy spirit to be angry: for anger resteth in the bosom of fools.

THE BIBLE

🔸

60

Ye call me master and obey me not, ye call me light and seek me not, ye call me way and walk me not, ye call me life and desire me not, ye call me wise and follow me not, ye call me fair and love me not, ye call me rich and ask me not, ye call me eternal and ye seek me not, ye call me noble and serve me not, ye call me mighty and honor me not, ye call me just and fear me not. If I condemn ye, blame me not.

*Engraved on an old slab, Lübeck, German Cathedral*

※

The fields are damaged by weeds, mankind is damaged by hatred; therefore a gift bestowed on those who do not hate brings great rewards.

*Buddhist Canon*

※

There is no fault in those who believe and do deeds of righteousness — God loves the good doers.

THE QUR'AN

※

The vile are ever prone to detect the faults of others, though they be as small as mustard seeds, and persistently shut their eyes against their own, though they be as large as vilva fruits.

THE PIRRANAS

✳

A man may pray to Ahura Mazda (God) to make him better, to make him happier, but not for evil to befall an enemy.

*Zoroastrian Faith*

✳

Let a man overcome anger by mildness, let him overcome evil by good; let him overcome the niggard by liberailty, the liar by truth!

*Buddhist Canon*

✳

Four classes of men will never see God's face: the scoffer, the liar, the slanderer, and the hypocrite.

THE TALMUD

✳

Rejoice not when your enemy falls, and let not your heart be glad when he stumbles.

THE BIBLE

✽

Get rid of your preachers and discard your teachers, and the people will benefit a hundredfold. Root out your schemers and renounce your profiteers, and thieving will disappear.

TAO TE CHING

✽

There are seven sins in the world: wealth without work, pleasure without conscience, knowledge without character, commerce without morality, science without humanity, worship without sacrifice, and politics without principle.

*Mahatma Gandhi*

✽

All sins, great and small, may be forgiven by repentance, except two: cowardice and theft.

*Shinto Faith*

✽

Attend to your prayers and pay the alms-tax. Your good works shall be rewarded by Allah. He is watching over all your actions.

THE QUR'AN

❋

The wealthy should aid the poor, remembering that the spirits are three feet above your head.

*Chinese Ethical Belief*

❋

You want no one to know it? Then don't do it.

*Chinese Proverb*

❋

A wicked man who reproaches a virtuous one is like one who looks up and spits at heaven; the spittle soils not the heaven, but comes back and defiles his own person.

*Buddha*

❋

A man is not just if he carries a matter out by violence; no, he who distinguishes both right and wrong, who is learned and leads others, not by violence but justly and righteously, and who is guarded by the law and is intelligent, he is called just.

*Buddhist Canon*

❋

In the heart of this phenomenal world, within all its changing forms, dwells the unchanging Lord. So go beyond the changing, and, enjoying the inner, cease to take for yourself what to others are riches.

THE UPANISHADS

❋

When the government is muddled and confused, the people are genuine and sincere. When the government is discriminate and clear, the state is crafty and cunning. Disaster is that on which good fortune depends. Good fortune is that in which disaster is concealed, who knows where it will end? For there is no fixed "correct." The "correct" turns into the "deviant," and "good" turns into "evil." People's state of confusion has certainly existed for a long time. Therefore be square but don't cut. Be sharp but don't stab. Be straightforward but not unrestrained. Be bright, but don't dazzle.

TAO TE CHING

Therein the being followeth likes and dislikes and findeth ne'er the time to know equality. Avoid, O my son, likes and dislikes. If you realize the emptiness of all things, compassion will arise within your hearts, if ye lose all differentiation between yourselves and others, fit to serve others you will be. And when serving others ye shall win success, then shall ye meet with me and finding me, ye shall attain to Buddhahood.

*Milarepa*

Demonic men do not understand either acting or turning away. In them there is no purity, or even good conduct or truth. They say the world is without reality, without foundation, without a Lord, not made by one thing following another but only moved by desire.

*Buddhist Canon*

# Love's Flowers

One who pervades the great universe is seen by none unless a man knows the unfolding of love.

*Sahaja Sect, Tantra, Bengal*

✷

Thus, with the hatred dispelled, he should direct thoughts of love toward his enemy just as he does toward a dear person.

*Buddhist Faith*

✷

This is the sum of all righteousness: in causing pleasure or in giving pain, in doing good or injury to others, a man obtains a proper rule of action by looking at his neighbor as himself.

MAHABHARATA

✷

I do not ask of you a wage for this, except love for the kinfolk; and whosoever gains a good deed, we shall give him increase of good in respect of it.

THE QUR'AN

✵

With thy sweet soul, this soul of mine
hath mixed as water doth with wine.
Who can the wine and water part,
or me and thee when thou art
become my greater self;
small wounds no more can me confine.
Thou hast my being taken on,
and shall not I now take on thine.
Thy love hast pierced me through and through.
Its thrill with bone and nerve entwine.
I rest a flute laid on thy lips;
a lute, I on thy breast recline.
Breathe deep in me that I may sigh;
yet strike my strings, and tears shall shine.

*Rumi*

✵

Praised be my Lord for all those who pardon one another for His love's sake, and who endure weakness and tribulation; blessed are they who peaceably shall endure, for Thou, O most high, shall give them a crown.

*St. Francis*

❋

It was the Sermon on the Mount, rather than a doctrine of passive resistance, that initially inspired the Negroes of Montgomery to dignified social action. It was Jesus of Nazareth that stirred the Negroes to protest with the creative weapon of love.

*Dr. Martin Luther King. Jr.*

❋

Because thou lovest the burning ground,
O dark one,
I have made a burning ground of my heart.

*Adapted from a Bengali Hymn*

❋

71

The Bible charges us to love our neighbors and our enemies, probably because they are the same people.

*G.K. Chesterton*

※

Love . . . by itself makes light everything that is heavy and bears evenly all that is uneven. For it carries a burden that is no burden, and everything that is better it makes sweet and tasteful . . . Love feels no burden, thinks nothing of trouble, attempts what is above its strength, pleads no excuse of the impossible. . . . Though weary it is not tired, though pressed it is not straightened; though alarmed, it is not confounded; but like a lively flame and burning torch forces its way upward and securely passes through all. . . . In whatever instance we seek ourselves there we fall from love.

*Thomas à Kempis*

※

Hear, O Israel! The Lord your God is one. And you shall love your Lord God with all your heart and with all your soul and with all your might. And these words which I command you this day shall be in your heart.

*Moses*

❋

Though I speak with the tongues of men and angels, and have not charity, I am become as sounding brass, or a tinkling cymbal. And though I have the gift of prophecy, and understand all mysteries, and all knowledge; and though I have all faith, so that I could remove mountains, and have not charity, I am nothing. And though I bestow all my good to feed the poor, and though I give my body to be burned, and have not charity, it profiteth me nothing.

St. Paul

❋

Love is patient and kind; it is not jealous or conceited or proud; love is not ill-mannered or selfish or irritable; love does not keep a record of wrongs; love isn't happy with evil, but is happy with the truth. Love never gives up; and its faith, hope, and patience never fail. . . . It is love then that you should strive for.

*St. Paul*

❋

Be watchful, stand firm in your faith, be courageous, be strong. Let all that you do be done in love.

THE BIBLE

❋

Make us worthy, Lord, to serve our fellow men throughout the world who live and die in poverty and hunger. Give them through our hands this day their daily bread, and by our understanding and love, give peace and joy.

*From the Daily Prayer*
*of the Co-Workers of Mother Theresa*

❋

Hear again the most secret doctrine of all, my ultimate word. Because I greatly desire thee, therefore shall I tell thee thy salvation. Think on me, worship me, sacrifice to me, pay me homage, so shalt thee come to me. I promise thee truly I love thee well. Give up all things of the world and turn to me as thy refuge. I will deliver thee from all evil. Have no care.

*Krishna's Secret Doctrine, Hindu Faith*

※

God has two dwellings; one in heaven, and the other in a meek and thankful heart.

*Isaak Walton*

※

But I say unto you, love your enemies, bless them that curse you, do good to them that hate you, and pray for them which spitefully use you.

THE BIBLE

※

# Death's Doorway

The mind-moon is solitary and perfect. The light swallows the ten thousand things. It is not that light illuminates objects, nor are these objects in existence. But when both light and objects are gone, what is it that remains?

*Zen Poem*

✱

To everything there is a season, and a time to every purpose under the heaven; a time to be born, and a time to die; a time to plant, and a time to pluck up that is planted.

The Old Testament

✱

Charity doth deliver from death, not merely from unnatural death, from death itself.

The Talmud

✱

This is the place of the infinite spirit. Achieving it, one is freed from delusion. Abiding in it, even at the time of death, one finds the pure calm of infinity.

THE BHAGAVAD-GITA

✦

Life is a journey. Death is a return to the earth. The universe is like an inn. The passing years are like dust. Regard this phantom world as a star at dawn, a bubble in a stream, a flash of lightning in a summer cloud, a flickering lamp. A phantom, a dream!

*Buddha's Advice*

✦

Jesus told her, "I am the one who raises the dead and gives them life again. Anyone who believes in me, even though he dies like anyone else, shall live again. He is given eternal life for believing in me and shall never perish."

THE BIBLE

✦

Gilgamesh said: "O barmaid, let me not see the death I constantly fear! The barmaid said to him, "Gilgamesh, where are you wandering to? You will not find the life you seek. When the gods made mankind, they set death aside for men, but they kept life in their own hands. So Gilgamesh, do fill your belly, be happy day and night, take pleasure everyday; day and night, dance and play, wear clean clothes, wash your head, bathe in water, attend to the child who holds your hand. Let your wife be happy with you. This is what man's lot is."

*Babylonian, 400 BC*

✦

When that which is coming comes . . . and no soul shall then deny its coming, some shall be abased and others exalted. . . . There they shall hear no idle talk, no sinful speech, but only the greeting, peace . . . peace.

THE QUR'AN

✦

Just surrender to the cycle of things, give yourself to the waves of the great change, neither happy nor yet afraid, and when it is time to go, simply go, without any unnecessary fuss.

TAO TE CHING

❋

Those who are dead are never gone, they are there in the thickening shadow. The dead are not under the earth, they are in the tree that rustles. They are in the wood that grows, they are in the water that runs, they are in the water that sleeps. They are in the hut, they are in the crowd. The dead are not dead. Those who are dead are never gone, they are in the breast of the woman, they are in the child who is wailing and in the firebrand that flames. The dead are not under the earth, they are in the fire that is dying, they are in the grasses that weep. They are in the whimpering rocks, they are in the forest, they are in the house. The dead are not dead.

*Spirit Prayer from* CHANTS D'OMBRE

❋